MW01527410

GRADE **1** ONE

POWERTHINK

Cooperative Critical Thinking Activities

Written by Anita Reith Stohs

Illustrated by Becky J. Radtke

Editor: Hanna Otero

Cover Design: Kristin Lock

Graphic Artists: Danielle Dela Cruz and Anthony Strasburger

Note on reproduction of this material: No part of this publication may be reproduced, stored in a retrieval system, or transmitted, in any form or by any means—electronic, mechanical, recording, or otherwise—without prior permission of the publisher. Reproduction of workbook activity pages by classroom teacher for use in the classroom and not for commercial sale is permissible. Reproduction of these materials for an entire school system is strictly forbidden.

FS112110 POWERTHINK–Grade One
All rights reserved-Printed in the U.S.A.
Copyright ©2000 Frank Schaffer Publications
23740 Hawthorne Blvd., Torrance, CA 90505

Table of Contents

INTRODUCTION

"There are one-story intellects, two-story intellects and three-story intellects with skylights. All fact collectors who have no aim beyond their facts are one-story people. Two-story people compare, reason, generalize, using the labor of the fact collectors as their own. Three-story people idealize, imagine, predict – their best illumination comes from above through the skylight."

Oliver Wendell Holmes

As educators, our goal is to assist students to become "third-story thinkers." Both the National Council of Teachers of Mathematics and the National Science Teachers Association recommend including problem solving and decision making as major goals of education.

What is critical thinking? Research indicates that the skill most basic to critical thinking is the ability to listen or read actively while continuously analyzing the information being presented. Sounds pretty basic, doesn't it? This ability requires the learner to be able to engage in an internal dialogue. Effective learners can dialogue internally without skipping steps.

Current recommendations suggest that children can best learn critical thinking skills by working in small groups or pairs. Working in pairs forces students to externalize their thinking – to think aloud, and to identify errors and skipped steps. It also teaches students to recognize and edit unsystematic thinking in themselves and others.

The **POWERTHINK** series of reproducible activity sheets is designed to provide cooperative learning opportunities for either small groups or pairs. There are six levels of challenge in the **POWERTHINK** series, allowing you to introduce critical thinking material at a sequential pace.

This **POWERTHINK** book provides you with activity sheets that pertain to the major content areas of language arts, social studies, mathematics, science, art, and problem solving.

Levels 1, 2, and 3 of the **POWERTHINK** series are designed clearly and simply:

The Power Play symbol indicates the directions to the students. The icon shows two students working together, but small groups of three will work in many cases.

The Lightning Strike icon indicates extended activities to guide your students to further observations or academic destinations.

Under the dashed line on each activity sheet you will find the Power Up icon. These are the author's comments and directions to the educator on how to prepare the children for the activity. When you're ready to make copies of the activity sheets for your students, simply fold back on the dashed lines and this section will not appear on your student copies.

The teaching of critical thinking skills can also be a forum for truly individual positive reinforcement, so on page 63 you will find a list of powerful verbal reinforcers. Use these to encourage your students to become "**POWERTHINKERS.**"

Happy **POWERTHINKING!**

PLAY BALL!

Power Play

1. Look at each ball and think about how you have seen it used.
2. Tell how each ball is used.
3. Draw a line from each ball to the picture of how it is used.

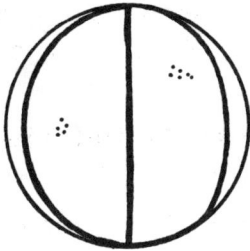

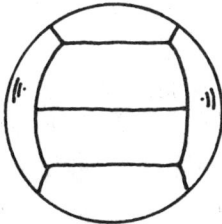

Lightning Strike!

Stick round stickers onto paper. Pretend the stickers are balls and draw children playing other kinds of games with them. Make up your own games!

Power Up!

Provide each group with a pencil.

CLEAN-UP TIME

Power Play
1. Talk about where Ramon's toys should go on his toy shelf.
2. Take turns drawing a line from each toy to where it goes.

Lightning Strike!
Draw a toy shelf onto a large piece of paper. Trace toy shapes onto the toy shelves. Take turns fitting the toys onto their shapes.

Power Up!
- Read the following aloud to the students: "Ramon has to clean up his room. All of his toys have to go back to their place on a shelf before Ramon can go out to play. Can you help him?"
- Provide each group with a pencil.

Frank Schaffer Publications

WHAT'S BEHIND THAT DOOR?

Power Play

1. Cut out each door at the bottom of the page.
2. Fold each door along the dotted line.
3. Glue each door to the blank square above.
4. Draw what is behind each door.

Example

closed   opened

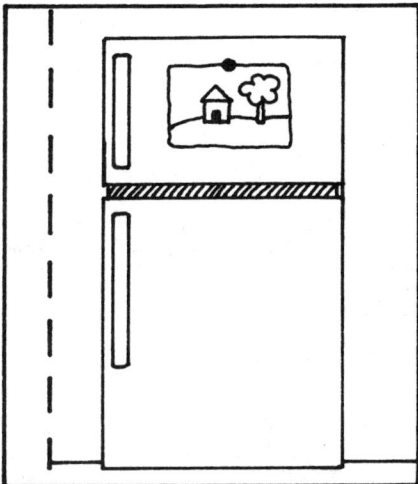  

Lightning Strike!

Cut paper into pages for a book. Make a door on each page. Draw something behind each door. Put the pages together. Write a title for the book. Give the door book to someone else to read.

- -

Power Up!

- Show how to cut and then fold a door along a dotted line. Glue the tab onto a piece of paper, then demonstrate how the door can open and close.
- Provide each group with scissors, glue, and crayons.

WHAT NEXT?

Power Play

1. Tell your partner what is happening in each picture.
2. Talk about what will happen next.
3. Draw what will happen next in the empty box next to each picture.

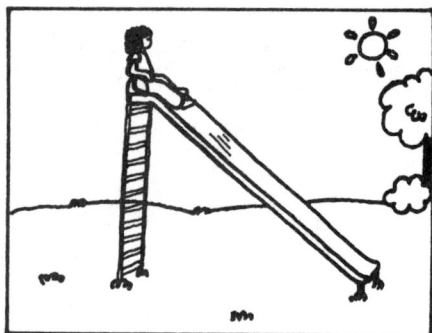

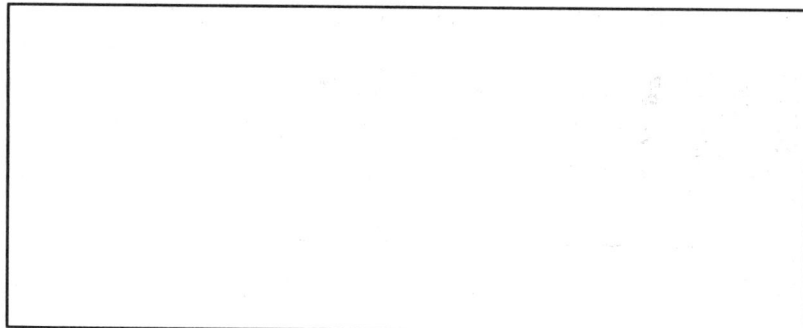

Lightning Strike!

Cut pictures from magazines. Glue each one to an index card. Take turns picking a card and predicting what will happen next.

Power Up!

- Explain that to **predict** means to decide what will happen next.
- Provide each group with crayons.

PUZZLE TIME

Power Play

1. Decide what kind of lines you want to draw.
2. Draw two lines on your puzzle.
3. Color each piece.
4. Cut out the pieces.
5. Take turns putting the puzzle together.

Like this!

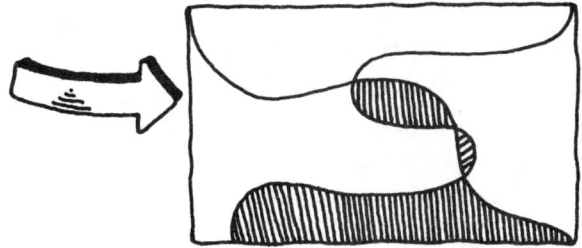

Lightning Strike!

Look at the three puzzle pieces below. A piece is missing. Draw the fourth piece to complete the puzzle.

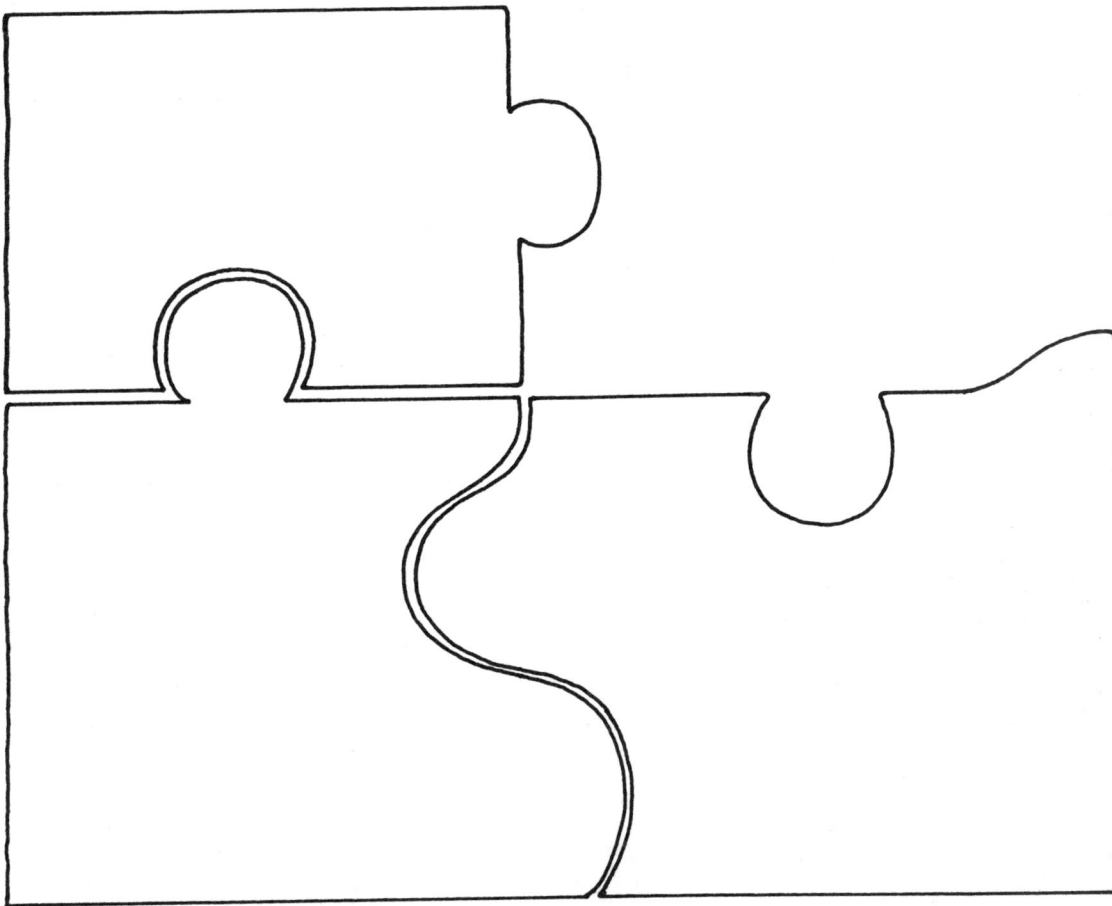

You'll do great!

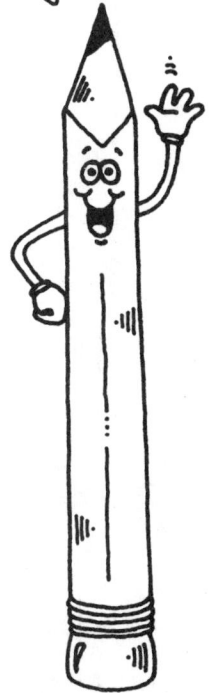

Power Up!

- Demonstrate the activity described above. Show that the two lines can go in the same direction or in different directions.
- Review different kinds of lines: straight, jagged, curved, and wavy.
- Provide each group with paper, crayons, and, scissors.

FS112110 POWERTHINK   Frank Schaffer Publications

DOT-TO-DOT-TO-DOT-TO-DOT!

Power Play
Take turns:
1. Look at each pattern.
2. Draw the rest of each pattern.

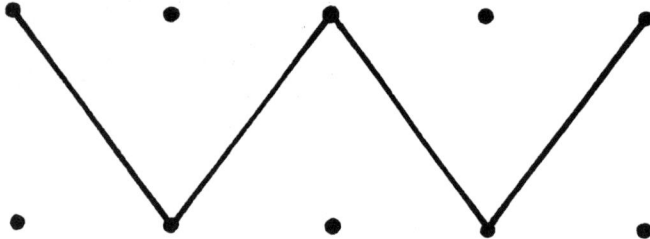

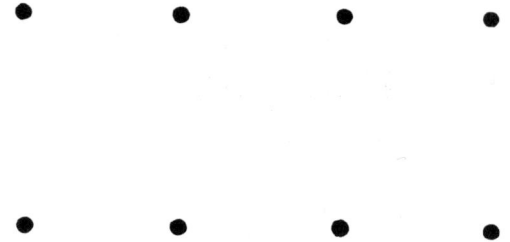

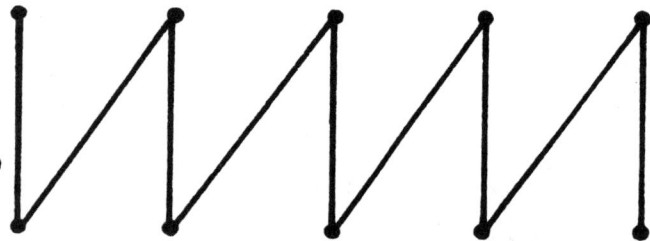

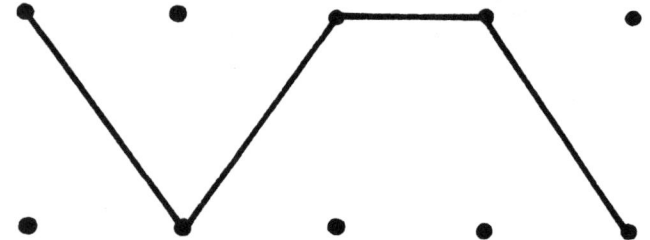

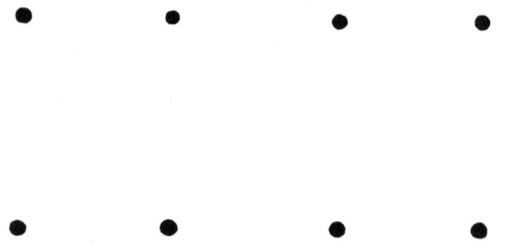

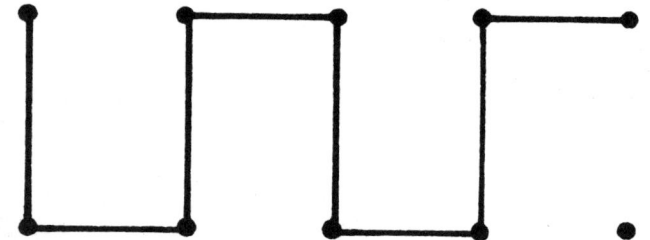

1.

2.

3.

4.

Lightning Strike!
Draw rows of dots. Start a pattern. Ask someone else to finish it.

Power Up!
- Draw two rows of dots on the board. Start a pattern. Have students tell you how to finish it.
- Provide each group with a pencil.

SCRAMBLED EGGS

Power Play

1. In each nest, find the egg that is different.
2. Find the nest where the egg belongs. Draw a line from the egg to the right nest.

Lightning Strike!

Make an egg matching game. Draw an egg on each half of an index card. Draw the same pattern on each egg. Cut the index cards in half. Make several sets of eggs. Take turns matching the eggs that are the same.

- -

Power Up!

- Read the following story to students: "The Cluck sisters did it again. Those feather-brained sisters forgot which nest was which. Now their Easter eggs are all mixed up. Help Henny, Penny, and Zenny put their scrambled eggs back."
- Review the concepts of "same" and "different."
- Provide a pencil for each group.

FS112110 POWERTHINK

Frank Schaffer Publications

INVENTIONS!

Power Play

1. Look at the pictures below. Do you see some familiar things?
2. Cut the pieces out and arrange them to create three objects that you are familiar with.

Lightning Strike!

Now look at the parts again. Arrange them to create a new invention. Write the name of your new invention. What does it do? How does it work?

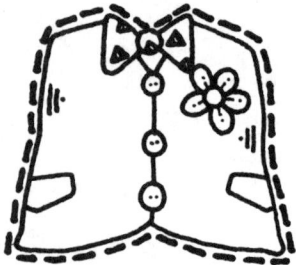

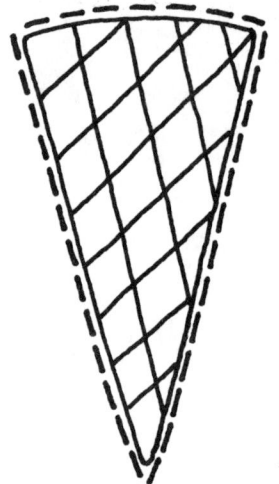

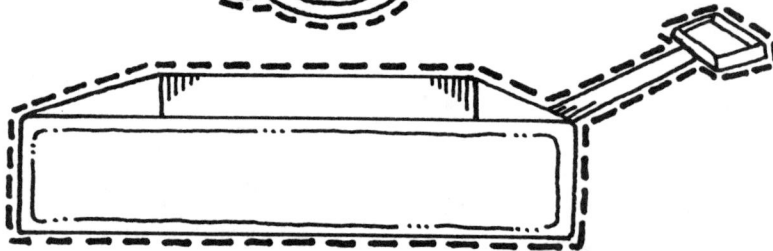

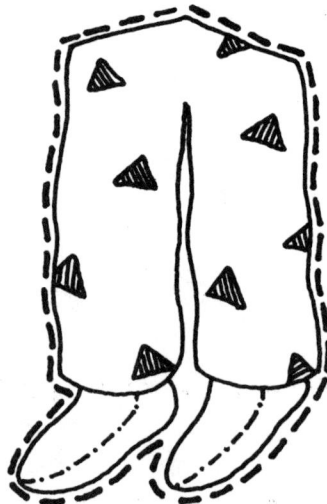

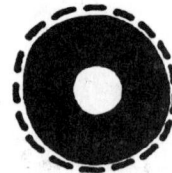

Power Up!

- Explain that inventors combine objects in new ways to make new inventions.
- Provide each group with crayons, scissors, pencils, glue, and a sheet of paper to glue their "parts" on.
- This page provides your students with a good synthesis activity. After first analyzing and assembling the parts to create something familiar, students move sequentially into synthesis as they create something totally new.

THE "GIRATRUNK"

Power Play

1. Pick two animals.
2. In the space below, draw a new animal made from parts of each animal.
3. Give the animal a name.
4. Tell where the animal lives, what it eats, what kind of sound it makes, and anything else you can think of.

(Part giraffe and part elephant:)

Lightning Strike!

Make up more new animals. Cut them out and stand them up in a box. Call your box the "New Zoo."

Power Up!

- Write "giraffe" and "elephant" on the board. Ask students to tell what kind of new animal they could make with parts from both of them.
- Show students the picture of the "Giratrunk."
- Provide each group with crayons.

Name(s)_____

ICE CREAM SURPRISE

Power Play
1. Look at the list of things that can go in an ice-cream sundae.
2. Make a sundae that you and your partner can share. Each of you can pick one flavor of ice cream and one topping to go into the sundae.
3. Draw a picture of your sundae and describe how to make it.

Ice Creams
vanilla
chocolate
strawberry
peppermint bon bon
fudge ripple
butter brickle

Toppings
caramel
whipping cream
chocolate syrup
peanuts
pineapple chunks
hot fudge
cherry

Draw your sundae in here...

Lightning Strike!
Make up new recipes with different kinds of foods. Draw pictures of what the new dishes would look like. Put the recipes together in a "New Food Cook Book."

Power Up!
- Talk with the students about how to make an ice-cream sundae. The goal is to break the sundae down into ingredients—such as the bowl, ice-cream, and toppings—and processes—such as getting a bowl, scooping out the ice-cream, and sprinkling on the toppings.
- Invite students to write down the responses they hear, or you can keep track of them on the board for all to see.
- Divide students into groups of two and provide each group with crayons.

SLOW-POKE RACE

Power Play

1. Look at the ways Snail and Turtle can go.
2. Draw a line from each animal to the finish.
3. Which one will get to the finish line last?_____
4. Tell why.

Lightning Strike!

Make up your own paths for the next race between Snail and Turtle.

Power Up!

- Read the following aloud to the students: "Snail and Turtle both move very slowly. They like to have races to see who moves the slowest. But whenever they race each other, they tie. Snail and Turtle must move at the same speed. This time, they will travel by different routes to reach the finish. The winner will be the one who takes the longest time to reach the finish."

Frank Schaffer Publications

WHAT'S DIFFERENT?

Power Play

Right now, the pairs of objects below don't match. With your partner, add lines to make each set of objects look the same.

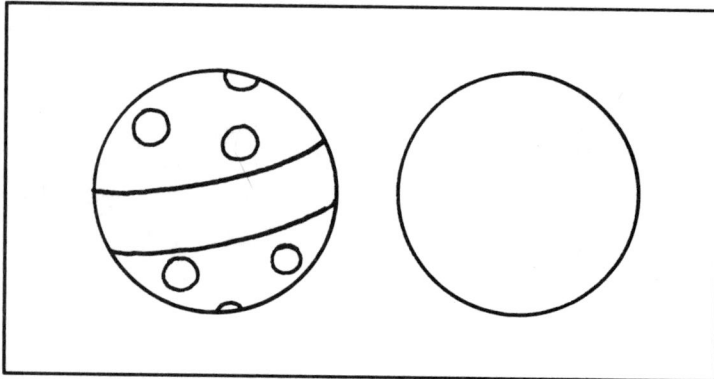

Lightning Strike!

Look at the two bugs below. With your partner, talk about the things that make them different.

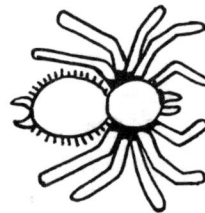

Power Up!

Critical thinking involves paying attention, and paying attention is a skill that needn't be limited to just listening. This simple and fun exercise will hone your students' observation skills and help them to pay attention to visual details.

- Provide each group with a pencil.

FS112110 POWERTHINK

TROLL TALE

Power Play
1. Look at the picture at each end of the time line.
2. What else happened in the story? Draw the pictures along the time line to show what happened.

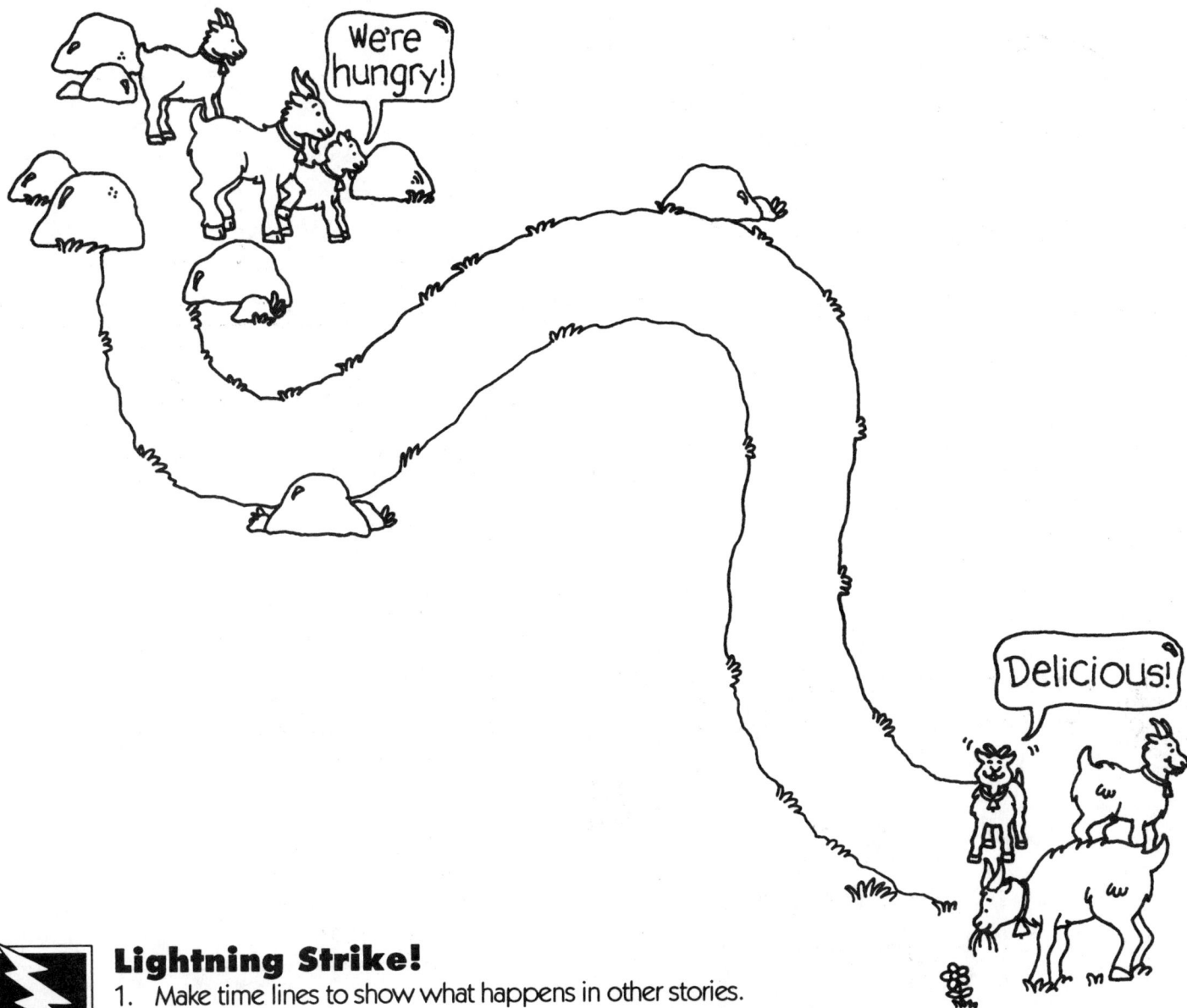

We're hungry!

Delicious!

Lightning Strike!
1. Make time lines to show what happens in other stories.
2. Draw pictures on a roll of paper. Unroll the paper as you tell the story.

- -

Power Up!
Students demonstrate their comprehension of a story by summarizing the order of events in a time line.
- Review or re-read the story of "The Three Billy Goats Gruff" with students.
- Explain that a "time line" is a line that shows when things happen.

Frank Schaffer Publications

"TRIP-TROP" THEATER

Power Play

1. Color and cut out the puppets.
2. Glue a stick to each puppet.
3. Decide who will move and talk for each puppet.
4. Tell the story to someone else.

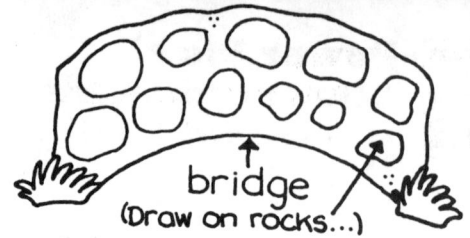

bridge
(Draw on rocks...)

Lightning Strike!

1. Make "props," like a bridge, from construction paper.
2. Draw your own puppets for another story.

puppet

Power Up!

Students demonstrate their comprehension of a story by translating it into the form of a puppet show.

*   Review or re-read the story of "The Three Billy Goats Gruff."
*   Set out scissors, glue, crayons, and four craft sticks.

Name(s)_____

SUPPER AT THE SPRATS'

Power Play

1. What foods could Jack and his wife eat? Write the names of foods they would want.

Jack Sprat	Ma Sprat
_____	_____
_____	_____
_____	_____
_____	_____
_____	_____

2. Draw food on each plate.

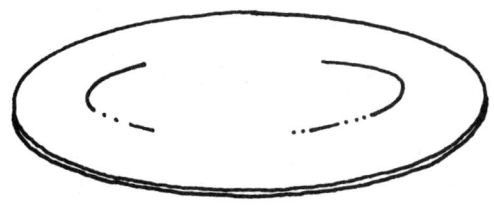

Jack Sprat could eat no fat,
His wife could eat no lean,
And so between the two of them,
They licked the platter clean.

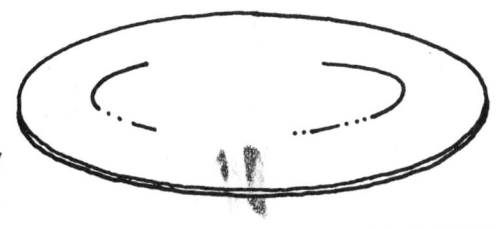

Power Up!
This two-part activity requires the student to read the rhyme to determine what types of foods Jack Sprat and his wife could eat and apply these criteria to categorize foods as "Jack Sprat" foods or "Ma Sprat" foods.
- Read through the poem with students.
- Explain the words "fat" and "lean."
- Set out crayons or markers.

FS112110 POWERTHINK   Frank Schaffer Publications

Name(s)_____

PICTURE PAIRS

Power Play
1. Work together to help the partners find each other.
2. Take turns telling why they go together.

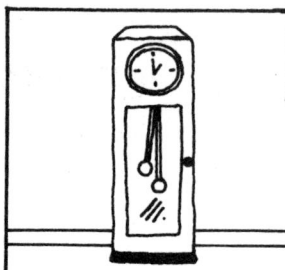

Lightning Strike!
1. Make up a story about how the characters lost their partners.
2. Take turns telling what will happen next to each pair.
3. Work together to make a poster of nursery rhyme partners.
4. Draw pictures of book partners lost from each other.

Power Up!
Comprehension is exhibited by students demonstrating a basic understanding of subject matter. By matching nursery rhyme partners and telling why they go together, students demonstrate such an understanding.
- Make sure students are familiar with nursery rhymes used in this activity: *Hickory, Dickory, Dock*; *Mary Had a Little Lamb*; *Jack and Jill*; and *Little Miss Muffet*.
- Explain that these nursery rhyme characters have lost their partners and need help in finding each other.

Name(s)_____

A MIXED-UP MESS

Power Play
1. Help the story friends find their things. Cut out the squares.
2. On the following page, put the squares on the side that they belong.
3. Glue down the squares.

Little Red Hen

Bremen Town Musicians

Lightning Strike!
1. Talk with your partner about what other things the Little Red Hen and the Bremen Town Musicians might use. List them on the following page.
2. Draw pictures of some of these things next to the animals that would use them.

Power Up!
Categorizing is a basic analytical skill. Here, the students use what they know about two nursery rhymes to differentiate between musical instruments and kitchen utensils. After the activity, you might spark some creative thinking by discussing ways that some of the kitchen utensils could be used as musical instruments, and vice versa.
- Review or re-read the stories of "The Little Red Hen" and "The Bremen Town Musicians."
- Read the following introduction: "What a mix-up! When the Bremen Town Musicians came for dinner to the Little Red Hen's house, their musical instruments got mixed up with the Little Red Hen's cooking equipment. Sort out the mess."
- Provide each group with scissors and glue.

FS112110 POWERTHINK — Frank Schaffer Publications

Little Red Hen

Bremen Town Musicians

List some of the other things the Little Red Hen and the Bremen Town musicians might use here:

_____   _____
_____   _____
_____   _____
_____   _____
_____   _____
_____   _____

FS112110 POWERTHINK

SILLY SPORT

Power Play

Hey diddle, diddle,
The cat and the fiddle,
The cow jumped over the moon;
The little dog laughed
To see such sport,
And the dish ran away with the spoon.

1. Read "Hey Diddle Diddle."
2. Talk about what the word "silly" means. What is the silliest thing you've ever seen?
3. What silly things are in the rhyme? Underline them.
4. What is the silliest thing in the poem? Draw a picture of it.

5. Talk or write about what makes it so silly.

_____

_____

Lightning Strike!

Look for silly things in other rhymes. What things could and could not happen?

- -

Power Up!

To evaluate things for their silliness, students first have to establish what "silly" is. You may want to establish some simple "silly criteria" on the board before dividing the class into small groups.

TONGUE TICKLERS

Power Play

1. Read these tongue twisters. Try to say them as fast as you can.

   Big black bug
   She sells sea shells.
   Pat's pink pig

2. Pick a letter of the alphabet.
3. Make up your own tongue twisters. (Have all the words start with the same letter.)

   _____

   _____

4. Pick a new letter and make up some tongue twisters for that letter.

   _____

   _____

5. Try to say your tongue twisters. Put a star by the one you like best.

Laurie's little lamb limped on his left leg...

Lightning Strike!

1. Draw pictures to go with your tongue twisters.
2. Look at "tongue twister" books from your local library. An easy-to-read example is:
   Oh Say Can You Say? by Dr. Seuss. Try some of the tongue twisters in these books.

- -

Power Up!

This activity combines comprehension (recognizing letters and sounds) with synthesis (making up a phrase that is hard to say).

- Explain that a "tongue twister" is several words that are hard to say together very quickly, usually because they begin with the same sound.

Name(s)_____

GOLDILOCKS RETURNS

Power Play

1. Talk about what might happen if Goldilocks went back to the Three Bears' house.
2. Draw a picture of what might happen.

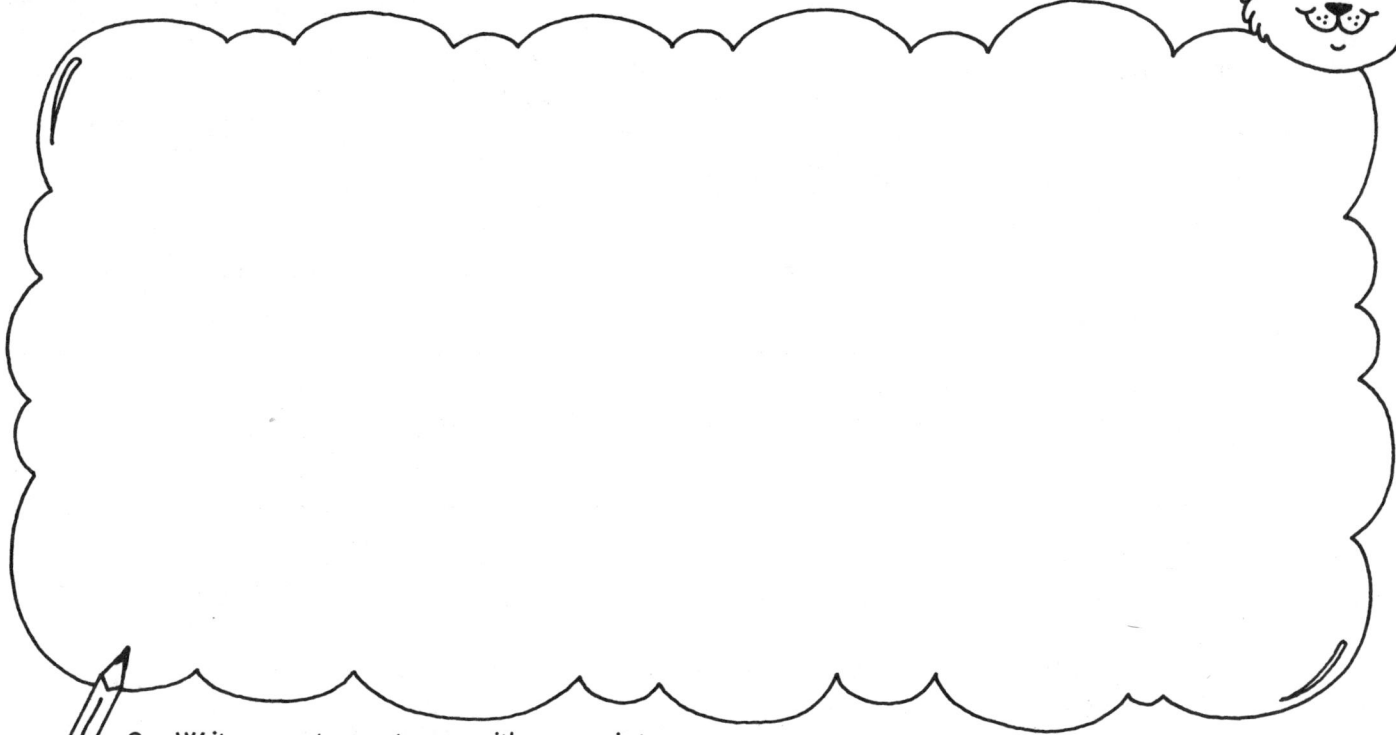

3. Write a sentence to go with your picture.

_____

_____

Lightning Strike!

Draw pictures to show what might happen next in other folk tales.

Power Up!

To predict the future, students must be able to combine their knowledge of what has already happened with a critical eye towards the range of possible outcomes. In this activity, students speculate on the fate of a Goldilocks who has not learned her lesson.

- Review or re-read the story of "Goldilocks and the Three Bears." Ask students to think about what would happen if Goldilocks ever went back to the Three Bears' house.
- Provide crayons for each group.

NEW KID ON THE BLOCK

Power Play

1. Write the names of storybook characters you like.
    Talk about them with your partner.
    Do you like any of the same characters?

    _____

    _____

    _____

2. What if one of these characters moved to your town or city?
    Who would you like to have come live near you?

    _____

3. Tell why.

    _____

    _____

    _____

Lightning Strike!

Draw a picture of you playing with the storybook person or animal you chose.

- -

Power Up!

Students evaluate storybook characters as neighbors. After choosing one character, they must think about their evaluation criteria to tell why they chose that particular character.

• Review recent stories you have read in class.

• Explain that a "character" is a person or animal in the story.

THAT COULDN'T HAPPEN HERE

Power Play

Our folk tale: _____

1. Take turns telling what could have really happened in the story and why. Draw a picture of one thing that could have happened.

> This could have happened...

2. Take turns telling what could not have happened in the story and why not. Draw a picture of one thing that could not have happened.

> This could not have happened!

Lightning Strike!

Tell about or draw a picture of the most unbelievable thing in the story.

Power Up!

Students need to learn to evaluate what they read. This activity asks them to think about what could and could not really happen in a story and give reasons why or why not.

- Have students tell how they know if something in a folk or fairy tale could have really happened.
- Ask each group to pick a folk or fairy tale.

WAYS TO HELP

Power Play

1. Draw a picture of your family.
2. Share your picture with someone else.
3. Talk about how the people in your family help one another.

Lightning Strike!

1. Write or draw a picture of each person in your family helping someone.
2. Find out how your family is like or different from other families.

- -

Power Up!

One way to begin thinking about how an organization works is to look at the roles played by each member of the organization. In this activity, students analyze and describe family members in terms of helping relationships.

- Talk about how different members of a family help each other.
- Provide crayons for each group.

WHERE WE LIVE

Power Play

1. Look at the pictures. Write a word from the word box at the top of the picture.

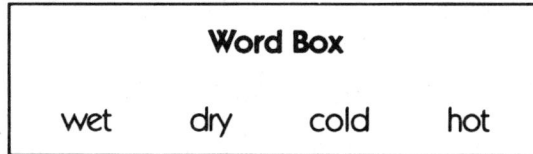

Word Box

wet   dry   cold   hot

2. Put a star by the place that is most like where you live.
3. Turn the paper over. Draw a picture of the place where your family lives. Draw your family in the picture.

Lightning Strike!

1. Draw pictures of places where you have been. Tell what they were like.
2. Draw a picture of a place where you would like to go. Tell what it would be like.

- -

Power Up!

This activity involves analysis and the application of prior knowledge. Students first analyze pictures, looking for clues in the pictures about the climate. They then demonstrate their comprehension of the words **wet, dry, cold,** and **hot.**

- Talk about places in the world that are wet, dry, cold, or hot.
- Provide crayons for each group.

NEIGHBORHOOD HELPERS

Power Play
1. Color and cut out the community helper puppets. Tape the ends together.
2. Take turns picking a puppet and showing what it does to help.

Mail Carrier

Fire Fighter

Police Officer

Librarian

Lightning Strike!
1. Draw puppets for other kinds of neighborhood helpers.
2. Make up a play about the helpers. Give the play to the class.

- -

Power Up!
- Review what the neighborhood helpers shown do to help us.
- Provide each group with crayons, scissors, and tape.

FOLLOW THAT MAP

Power Play

1. Look at the map of the shopping center.
2. Find the different parts of the shopping center.
3. Together follow these directions to the book store:
   a. Go to the table.
   b. Turn right.
   c. Go to the bench.
   d. Turn left.
   e. Go in store.
4. Take turns telling your partner how to go to different parts of the shopping center.

Lightning Strike!

1. Tell how a shopping center you have been to is the same or different from this shopping center.
2. Tell what you can buy or do in each part of the shopping center.

- -

Power Up!

Explain how to follow directions on a map.

HOME SWEET HOME

Power Play

1. Look at the pictures.
2. Talk about things that are the same for all the homes.
3. Write one thing that is the same for all the homes.

_____

4. Talk about things that are different about the homes.
5. Write one thing that is different about the homes.

_____

Lightning Strike!

Draw your own home. Tell what is the same or different about it compared to the houses in the picture.

- -

Power Up!

- Talk about how people around the world live in different kinds of homes.
- Review the meaning of "same" and "different."

DO YOU NEED THAT?

Power Play
1. Look at the pictures.
2. Decide, with your partner, if it is a need or a want.
3. Cross out the pictures that do not belong.

NEEDS

WANTS

Lightning Strike!
Cut or draw pictures to put on a poster showing needs and wants.

- -

Power Up!
Review the difference between things we need and things we want.

GET READY FOR A TRIP

Power Play
1. Pick a place in the world for your group to go.
2. Talk about what it would be like there. Would it be hot or cold, wet or dry?
3. Draw pictures of things you would need at that place.
4. Talk about why you would need them.

My group is going to visit

_____

When we get there it will be _____

Here are things I will need:

_____   _____

_____   _____

_____   _____

_____   _____

Lightning Strike!
Make a book showing the things you would need to visit different places.

What I Need When I Visit....
by Lisa R.

- -

Power Up!
- Talk about different places to go and the kinds of climates around the world.
- Provide each group with crayons.

THE BEST TIME OF THE YEAR

Power Play

1. Color the pictures of the seasons.
2. Talk with your partner about what you like to do in each season. Is there anything that you both like to do during one of the seasons?
3. Pick the season you like best. Draw a picture of it.
4. Show the picture to your partner. Tell why you like that season best.

Winter	Spring	Summer	Fall

My favorite season is _____!

Lightning Strike!

Make a poster showing you and your partner in every season.

Power Up!

• Talk about what you do during the different seasons in your part of the world.
• Provide crayons for each group.

35

MATCH THE NUMBERS

Power Play

1. Put the cards on the table.
2. Take turns matching the cards.

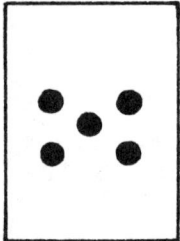

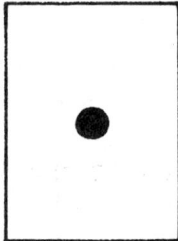

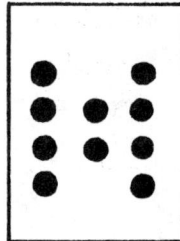

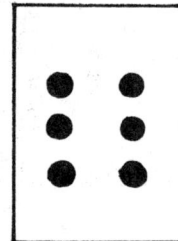

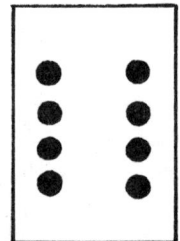

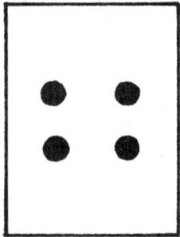

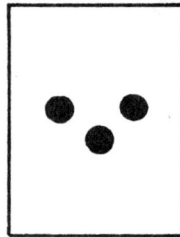

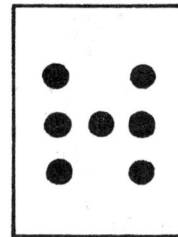

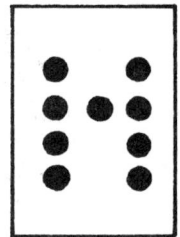

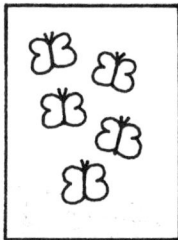

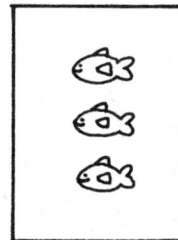

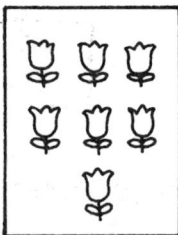

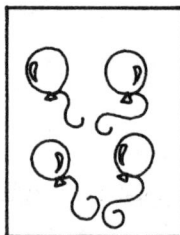

Fun!

Lightning Strike!

Write the words for each number on index cards. Match them to the other cards.

Power Up!

Children possess an intuitive sense of equivalence. This activity will reinforce that and allow them to build upon their prior knowledge. Take the activity one step further by preparing ten index cards numbered 1-10 for each student group . Have them match these cards to the others.

SCHOOL CARNIVAL

Power Play

1. Jessica is at the school carnival. She has this much money left to spend. How much does she have? _____

2. What can Jessica buy? Take turns looking at each picture. Put an **X** over what Jessica cannot buy.

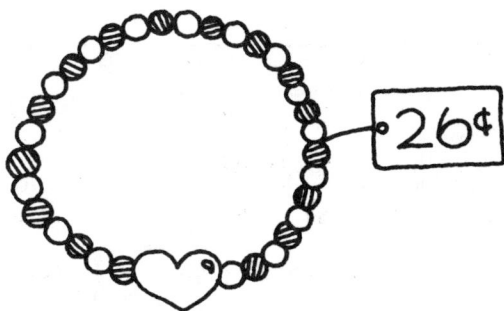

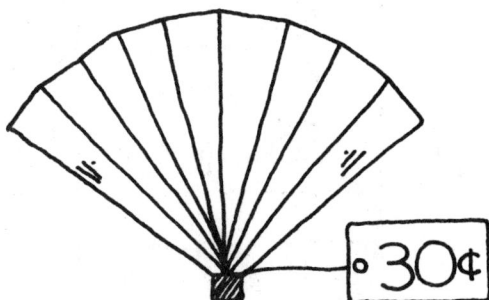

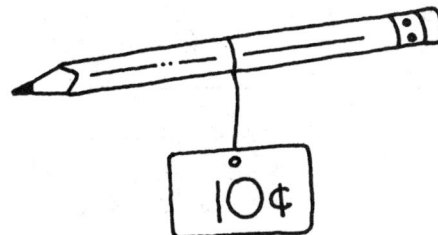

26¢

15¢

30¢

10¢

Lightning Strike!

Jessica wants to buy two things with her money. Circle the two things she can buy.

Power Up!

This activity requires students to think about whether an item's price is more or less than the amount of money available to spend. They are also asked to evaluate what combination of numbers will allow two items to be bought with the money available.

• Draw a ball with "2¢" written on it and a box with "6¢" written on it. Ask students to decide if a nickel would be enough to buy both items. Have students create a number sentence that will illustrate the problem.

SNACK STAND

Power Play

1. Look at Stephen's sign.
2. Look below to see the snack each friend bought.
3. Write a number sentence to show the cost of each snack.

juice - 5¢
cookie - 3¢
popcorn - 4¢

Tyrone_____

Joe_____

Katy_____

Amy_____

Tyrone bought....

Joe bought...

Katy bought...

Amy bought...

Lightning Strike!

What would you sell in a stand? Draw a picture to show it. Draw pictures of what your friends would buy. Make up number sentences to show the cost.

Power Up!

- Review how to solve story problems by writing number sentences.
- Read this introduction to students: "Stephen made a stand for selling snacks. In it he put apple juice, popcorn, and cookies. In front of the stand, he put a sign saying what each snack cost. His neighborhood friends came to buy from him."

NUMBER PATTERNS

Power Play
1. Look at the number trains.
2. Look for number patterns.
3. Take turns writing the numbers that fit on each car.

Train 1: | 1 | 2 | 3 | | 5 | |

Train 2: | 5 | 10 | | | 20 | 25 | |

Train 3: | | | 3 | 5 | 7 | |

Train 4: | | 4 | | | 8 | 10 |

Lightning Strike!
Think of your own number pattern. Draw a number train to show it.

- -

Power Up!
Young children spontaneously search out and use relationships to intelligently solve mathematical problems. **Playing** with numbers and encouraging students to discover and use their prior knowledge will help them to avoid blind procedure-following later on.

Frank Schaffer Publications

WAYS TO MAKE TEN

Power Play

1. What numbers can you add to make 10? Take turns writing number sentences. The first one is done for you.

1. __1__ + __9__ = __10__   2+

2. ____ + ____ = ____

3. ____ + ____ = ____

4. ____ + ____ = ____

5. ____ + ____ = ____

2. Pick another number. See how many ways you can add two numbers to make that number.

____ + ____ = ____   ____ + ____ = ____

____ + ____ = ____   ____ + ____ = ____

____ + ____ = ____   ____ + ____ = ____

____ + ____ = ____   ____ + ____ = ____

Lightning Strike!

See how many numbers you can subtract from 10 or another number.

Power Up!

Review addition of numbers that add up to 10.

WHO'S TALLEST?

Power Play
1. Who is the tallest: Chris, Mimi, or Matthew?
2. Chris says, "I am the shortest."
3. Matthew says, "I am taller than Mimi."
4. Draw a picture of each child.

draw!

Chris   Mimi   Matthew

Who is the tallest?_____

Lightning Strike!
Make up your own picture riddles. See if your partner can answer them.

- -

Power Up!
- Explain that drawing a picture is one way to solve a problem.
- Read: "Mimi, Chris, and Matthew want you to guess who is tallest."

GAME TIME

Power Play

1. Read what each child threw:
   - Amy threw a 2.
   - Weston threw a 5.
   - Kendra did not throw a 3.
   - Jeff threw a 4.
   - Ashley did not throw a 6.
2. First, cross out each number that Kendra did not throw.
3. What numbers are left?

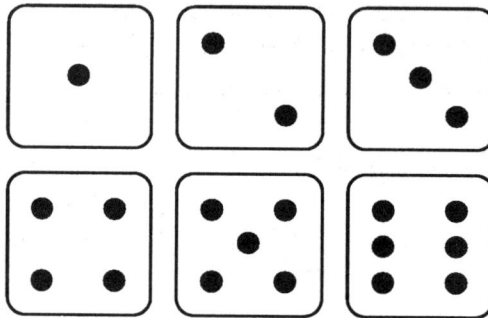

_____

4. If Kendra did not throw a 3, what number is left?_____
   That is the number that Kendra threw!

Did you guess what I threw?

Lightning Strike!

What if Amy threw a 6; Weston threw a 1; Kendra did not throw a 2; Jeff threw a 5; and Ashley did not throw a 4? What number did Kendra throw?

Power Up!

Read the following story to students: "Some neighborhood friends are playing a board game. Their names are Amy, Weston, Ashley, Jeff, and Kendra. They are throwing a die. The die has the numbers 1 through 6. Everyone threw a different number. No one threw a 1. What number did Kendra throw?"

Name(s)_____

Power Play

1. Trace your foot on the paper. Cut it out.
2. You will use the paper foot to measure the length of the blackboard. Estimate how long the blackboard is.

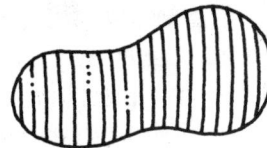

   The blackboard is about _____ paper feet long.

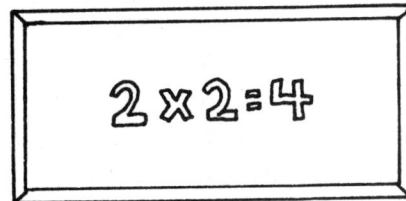

3. Measure the blackboard with your paper footprint.

   The blackboard is _____ paper feet long.

2 x 2 = 4

4. Compare your numbers with your partner's numbers. Did you measure the same number of paper feet? What made the numbers different?

5. Try the problems below. First estimate how long the objects are, then measure them. Compare your answers to your partner's.

   A. The teacher's desk is about _____ paper feet long.

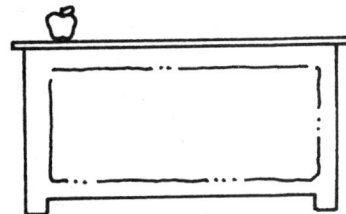

      The teacher's desk is _____ paper feet long.

   B. The coat rack is about _____ paper feet long.

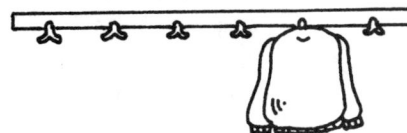

      The coat rack is _____ paper feet long.

   C. The bulletin board is about _____ paper feet long.

      The bulletin board is _____ paper feet long.

Lightning Strike!

Measure the blackboard with a ruler. How is the measurement different from your paper-foot measurement?

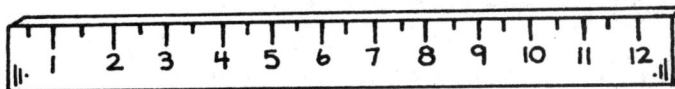

Power Up!

- Explain that the "foot" unit of measure was once based on the length of a king's foot.
- Explain that to estimate means to make a good guess.
- Supply construction paper, scissors, and a pencil for each group.

A FROG GROWS

Power Play
1. Cut apart the pictures.
2. Put the pictures in order. Glue them to the paper.
3. Talk with your partner about what is happening in the pictures.

1.	2.	3.

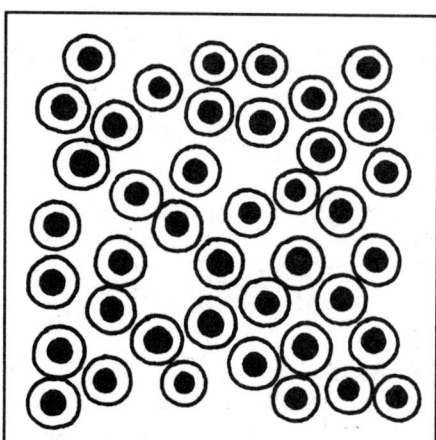

Lightning Strike!
1. Draw pictures that show how another animal grows. Mix them up and have someone else put them in order again.
2. Tell a story about what happens to the frog after it grows into an adult.

Power Up!
Science is filled with sequential processes. A seed germinates, grows into a plant, and produces new seeds. One thing leads to another. Encourage children to use their innate sense of sequence to place events in the correct order and predict the sequence of future events.
- Talk about how a frog grows from egg, to tadpole, to frog.
- Provide scissors and glue for each group.

Name(s)_____

WHO AM I?

Power Play
1. Pick an animal in the picture.
2. Think about where the animal lives, what sounds it makes, or what it does.
3. Say, "Who am I?" Tell one thing at a time about the animal until it is guessed.
4. Take turns guessing animals until all animals are named.

Lightning Strike!
Turn the paper over. Draw other types of things for each other to guess.

Power Up!
Children reason deductively when they apply a set of rules to solve a problem: "I know these are not my shoes because my shoes are blue, and these shoes are red." The rule is, "My shoes are blue." In this activity, the students make up the rules. First, a student analyzes a chosen animal, breaking it up into a set of attributes. The student's partner then uses these attributes, or rules, to make intelligent guesses about the identity of the secret animal.
- Explain the following game to the students: One partner picks an animal on the page, says "Who am I?" and gives a clue about it. The other partner tries to guess the name of the animal. Keep giving clues until the animal is guessed. Take turns guessing until all animals are named.

WHO LIVES HERE?

Power Play

1. Look at the pictures. Talk about what animal lives in each kind of home.
2. Draw a line between each animal and its home.

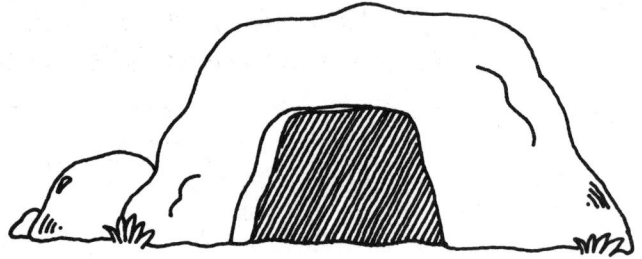

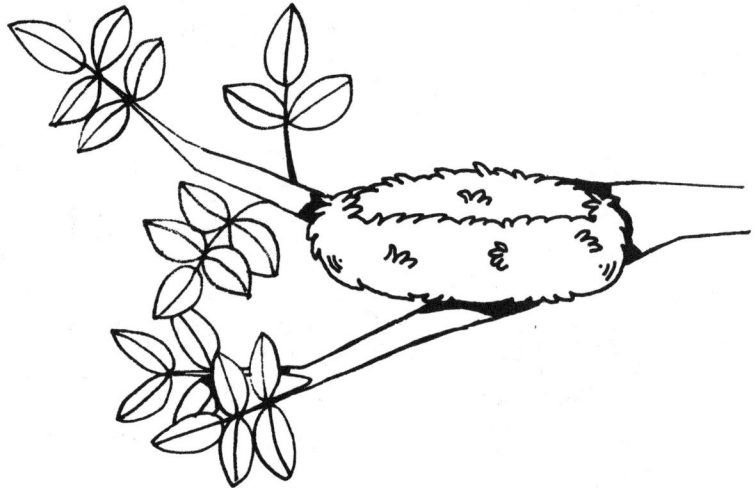

Lightning Strike!

Cut out pictures of animals. Draw pictures of the homes they live in.

- -

Power Up!

This activity encourages students to apply "old" knowledge to a new situation. They can use what they know about sizes, habits, and animal adaptations (such as wings) to help them solve a problem about something they may have no knowledge of: animal homes.

- Review the homes of different animals. Talk about how each animal is well suited to its home.
- Provide crayons for each group.

A FISH OUT OF WATER

Power Play

1. Does a rabbit live underwater? Find the rabbit and put an **X** on it.
2. Find other animals in the wrong place. Put an **X** on them.
3. How are all land animals alike? Talk about this with your partner.
4. Talk about what water animals have in common.

Lightning Strike!

Cut pictures of animals from magazines. With your partner, glue them onto big pieces of paper labeled "Land Animals" and "Water Animals."

Power Up!

When children reason inductively, they use a series of observations to reach a general conclusion: "The clock has struck twelve times at noon every day for the past week. That's how I know that the clock always strikes twelve times at noon." Here, students observe specific differences between land and water animals to reach some conclusions about how they differ in general.

- Talk about how some animals live on land and some live in the water.

FS112110 POWERTHINK — Frank Schaffer Publications

CLASS PET

Power Play

1. Pick an animal that would make a good class pet.
2. Draw the animal. Design a home for the animal. Don't forget the things that it needs to live.
3. Show your picture to the class. Tell about what you drew.

A Good Class Pet

Lightning Strike!

Put the pictures along the bulletin board. Vote on the animal the class would like best for a class pet.

- -

Power Up!

The first step in any creative thinking process is to identify the problem. The problem in this case: Design a home that meets the basic needs of a class pet. Designs for the pet's home can be whimsical or straightforward, as long as they meet the animal's basic needs.

- Review the care of different kinds of small animals often found in classrooms. Review the needs of all animals: shelter, food, and water.
- Provide crayons for each group.

CREATE CAMOUFLAGE

Power Play
1. Look at the animals. Each animal needs a camouflage pattern that will help it hide.
2. Color each picture, giving the animal a pattern that makes it hard to see.

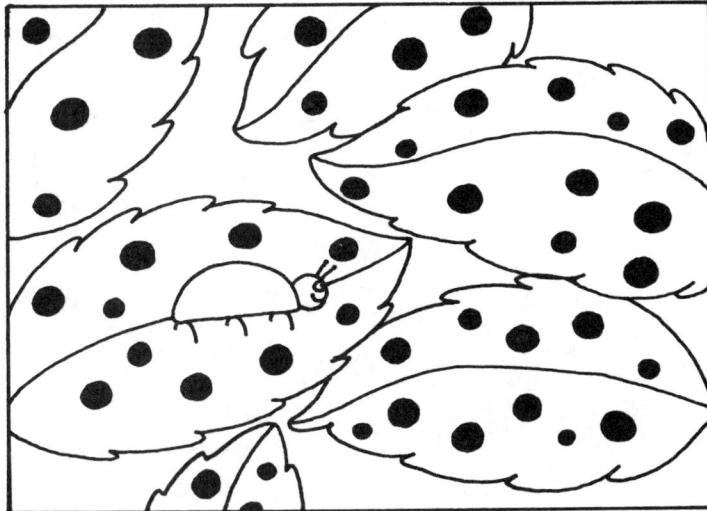

Lightning Strike!
Draw pictures of other animals with patterns. Tell how their patterns help them.

Power Up!
This is a creative thinking exercise with fairly strict boundaries. Students apply their knowledge of how camouflage works to design patterns for animals in their natural habitats.
- Talk about why animals have camouflage, and how patterns can make an animal hard to spot.
- Provide each group with crayons.

49

MY COLOR BOOK

Power Play

1. Number your pages 1 to 8.
2. Write "My Color Book" on page one.
3. Start on page three.
4. Write the name of a color on each page.
5. Pick out a crayon for each color.
6. Look around. Find things that match the colors in your book.
7. Draw a picture in your book to go with each color.
8. Read and show your book to the class.

Colors

red	yellow
blue	orange
green	purple

Print... My Color Book by Jana

then

Label each page a color... blue green

then

Look for things that are those colors. That raincoat is yellow!

Draw... red

then

Share with the class! And this is the last page. It's about purple!

Lightning Strike!

Make another color book. This time, think of a feeling that matches each color. Write the name of the feeling on each page. For each feeling, draw a picture.

Power Up!

- Review the primary and secondary colors: red, yellow, blue, orange, green, and purple.
- For each group, fold two sheets of paper and staple them in the center.
- Provide crayons for each group.

COLORS AND FEELINGS

Power Play

1. Look at the color names. Tell how each one makes you feel.
2. Draw a picture. Use colors that show how you feel about what you draw.
3. Tell about your picture when it is done.

Yellow makes me feel happy!

Colors					
red	yellow	blue	orange	green	purple

Lightning Strike!

Write each color word on a big piece of paper. Color a picture using only the color written on the page. Pass your color page to another group, and get a color page from a different group. Put all the pages together for a big book.

Power Up!

This activity requires students to make a creative leap: comparing a color to an emotion. This is a comparison that requires associative reasoning. Build on this exercise. If colors can communicate how you feel, what else, besides words, can also communicate how you feel?

• Provide each group with crayons, markers, or watercolors.

EYEDROPPER PAINTING

Power Play

1. Cover your desk with newspaper.
2. Put a paper towel over the newspaper.
3. What do you think will happen if you mix a dropper full of red and a dropper full of yellow on your paper towel?

_____

4. Try it. Look at your paper towel. What new color did you make?_____

5. What do you think will happen if you mix a dropper full of blue with a dropper full of red on your paper towel?

_____

6. Try it. Look at your paper towel. What new color did you make?_____

7. Can you predict what will happen if you mix a dropper full of blue with a dropper full of green on your paper towel?

_____

_____

7. Try it. Look at your paper towel. What new color did you make?

_____

(newspaper)   (paper towel)   (eye dropper)

Lightning Strike!

Drop colors onto coffee filters. Put them together on a large piece of paper for a flower mural.

- -

Power Up!

- Talk about how the three primary colors mix to make other colors.
- For each group, place a few drops of red, yellow, and blue food coloring in three cups of water.
- Provide eye droppers, construction paper, glue, newspaper, and white paper towels for each group.

MAKE A PATTERN

Necklace

Power Play
1. Put the macaroni on the yarn in a pattern.
2. Knot the ends of the yarn when you are done.
3. Color the beads below to match the beads you put on the yarn.
4. Look at the necklace your partner made.
5. Find what pattern your partner used.

Here's the color pattern I used to make my necklace.

Here's the color pattern my partner used.

Here's another color pattern I thought up.

Lightning Strike!
String necklaces from colored wooden or plastic beads.

Power Up!
- Color wide macaroni in three different colors of food coloring. Spread out on cookie sheet and let dry.
- Cut a 24" (61cm) piece of yarn for each student. Tape the ends to prevent fraying.
- Provide each group with a dish of different colored macaroni beads.
- Talk about different patterns the students can make as they combine the different colors.

LOUD OR QUIET!

Power Play

1. Talk with your partner about what makes a sound "loud" or "quiet."
2. Pick a sound that you like. It can be a loud sound or a quiet sound.
3. Choose colors that you think look like the sound you picked. For example, if you chose the sound of a siren (loud), you might pick the colors red and yellow because they are bright and catch your attention. If you chose the sound of water running in a stream (quiet), you might pick the colors blue and purple because they are calm and relaxing.
4. Tear pieces from the colors you chose and glue them below to make a "sound picture."

My Sound Picture

Lightning Strike!

Think about ways you could make a "loud" color quieter.

Power Up!

Provide each group with different colors of construction paper, scissors, and glue.

PICKING PICTURES

Power Play

1. Answer these questions:

   I like a picture of_____

   I like these colors in a picture: _____

2. Draw a picture with your partner. Pick colors you both like. Pick something to draw that you both like. Take turns drawing and coloring parts of the picture.

Lightning Strike!

Look at different art reproductions. With a partner, pick the one you like best. Explain why you like it. Draw your own picture by using the subject and colors in the picture you chose.

Power Up!

People like art for different reasons. This activity encourages students to begin to develop an understanding of how preferences in art can be based upon different criteria.

- Explain that people like different pictures for different reasons. Some like the colors in the picture, some like what the picture is about, and some like the way the picture is made. Ask students to share what they like in a picture.
- Provide crayons and a piece of paper for each group.

WHAT'S THE PROBLEM?

Power Play

A problem is a difficult situation that needs to be worked out. Everyone has problems. To solve a problem you need to find at least one answer. What if you missed the school bus? Would that be a problem? What if your dog chewed up your favorite toy? What if your TV broke?

1. You can't solve a problem if you don't know what it is to begin with.
2. Listen to the story as your teacher tells it.
3. In the box on the left, draw a picture of what the problem is.
4. In the box on the right, draw a picture of one way in which it could be solved.

The Problem	The Solution

Lightning Strike!

Talk with your partner about a problem you each have had recently. Draw pictures to show what they are and how they could be solved.

Power Up!

Read this to your students: Everyone else in the class is working away on a picture that your teacher asked you to draw. You've looked in your desk and on the floor, but you can't seem to find your pencil. What's the problem and what can you do about it?

Name(s)_____

PROBLEM SOLVING STRATEGIES

Power Play
1. Look at each picture.
2. Talk with your partner about what is happening.
3. Tell what the problem is.

It's mine!

gum   candy

4. What problem have you had? Draw a picture to show it.

Lightning Strike!
How do you think the children solved their problems? Draw pictures to show what they did.

Power Up!
- Talk with students about what the terms "problem" and "solve" mean.
- Explain that we solve a problem by first identifying what that problem is.

FS112110 POWERTHINK   Frank Schaffer Publications

ALLOWANCE TIME

Power Play

1. Look at the things in the store. Talk with your partner about what would be good or bad about each one.
2. Choose three things to buy. Circle them.
3. Tell someone else why you chose them.

Lightning Strike!

Draw a picture of things you have seen in a dollar store. Circle three things you would like to buy.

- -

Power Up!

- Sometimes it is hard to choose from among two or more options. Explain to students that one way to solve a problem like this is to think about the advantages and disadvantages of each option. Have them demonstrate this by first listing all the things they might do on a Saturday morning, and then talk about the good and bad points of each option.
- Tell the following story: "Pretend you get $3 from your aunt for your birthday. You take the money to the Dollar Store. Everything at the store costs one dollar. What will you buy?"

GOING TO GRANDMA'S

Power Play
Pretend that you are going to spend the night at your grandma's. You may take three toys along.

1. Write the names of toys you want to take.

   _____

   _____

   _____

   _____

   _____

   _____

2. Choose three toys to take.

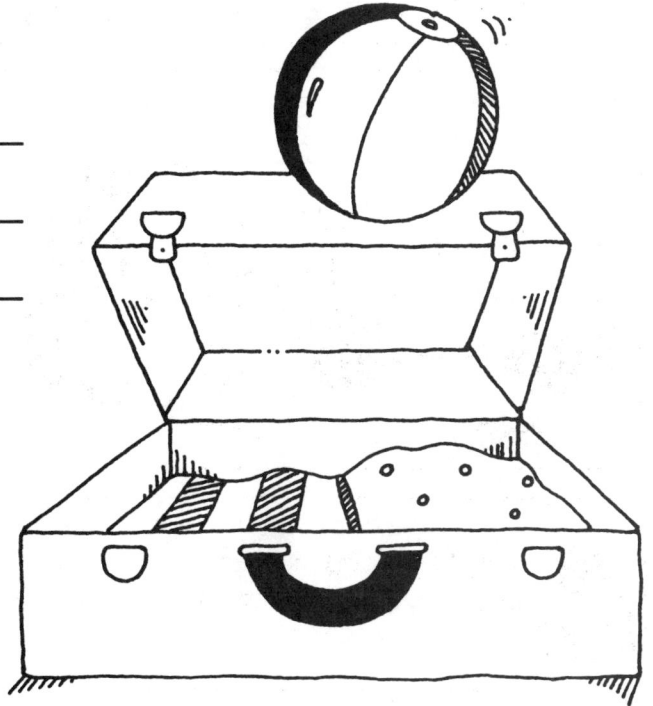

   _____

   _____

   _____

3. Tell your partner why you chose those toys.

Lightning Strike!
Draw the outline of a suitcase. Draw what you will need inside the suitcase for the overnight trip.

Power Up!
Explain that listing and making choices are important parts of problem solving.

FS112110 POWERTHINK — Frank Schaffer Publications

CHOOSING A BOOK

Power Play

1. Look at the books that your teacher has put in front of you. Look at the covers and open them up to take a peek at what's inside of each one.

2. Think about which one you would like to read first. Second? Third? Last? Write the titles of the books in the order you would like them read in class.

Book 1 _____

Book 2 _____

Book 3 _____

Book 4 _____

3. Compare your list with your partner's list. Are they the same? _____

4. If they are different, talk about how you can change your lists so that you are both happy.

Lightning Strike!

Write down the titles of any four books you like. Put them in the order you want them read to your class.

Power Up!

- Provide four picture books for each group.
- Demonstrate how to rank books by preference.

CHANGING MY ROOM

Power Play

1. Do you have a bedroom? Think about how you would like your room to look.
2. Draw a picture of how you would like your room to look. Where will the bed go? Where will the dresser go? Where is the door? Where is the window?

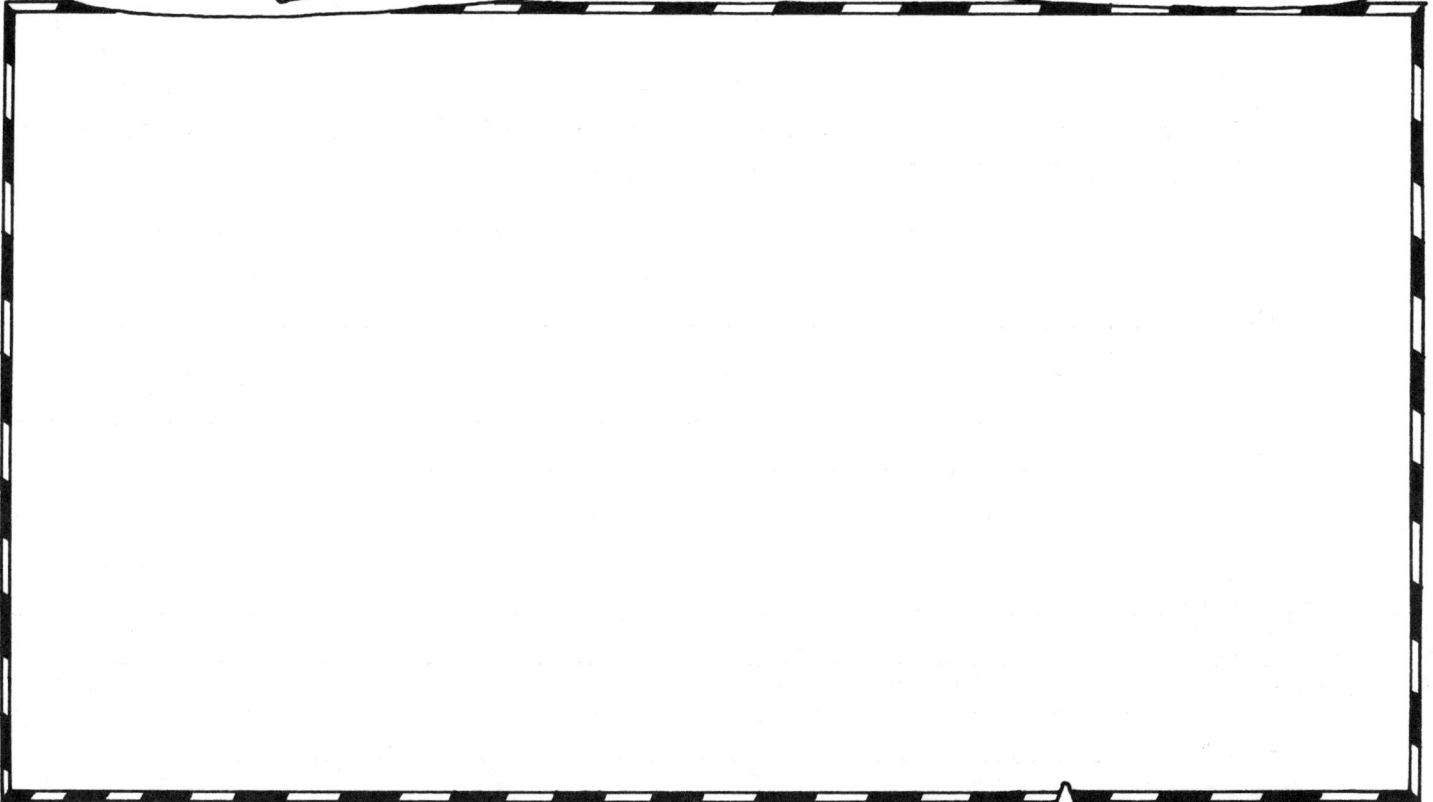

My Room ...

3. Show your picture to someone else.
4. Tell about how you want your room to look.

Lightning Strike!

Work together with your partner to draw a picture of how you want your classroom to look.

Power Up!

Explain to students that one way to solve a problem is to draw a picture of what you want to do.

WRAPPING PRESENTS

Power Play
1. Look at the presents Joe has to wrap. For each present, Joe has three boxes that might work.
2. Circle the box which Joe should use to wrap each present.

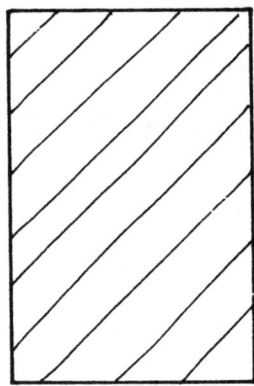

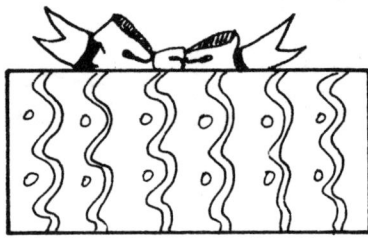

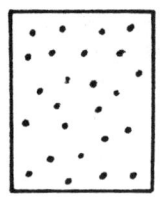

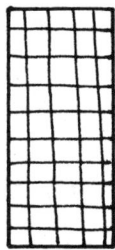

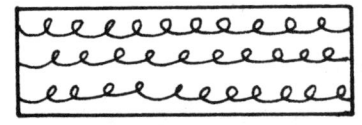

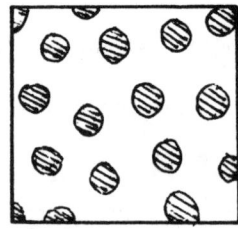

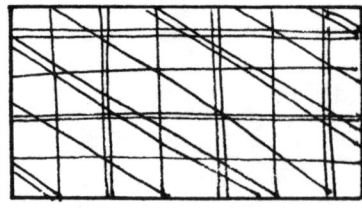

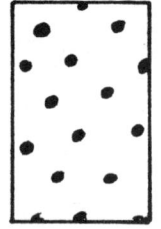

Lightning Strike!
What else could you estimate by size?

Power Up!
• Explain how estimating can help us make the right choice when solving a problem.
• Demonstrate to students that one way we can estimate is by size.

ENCOURAGING POWERTHINKING

One of the additional benefits of teaching critical thinking and problem solving in your classroom is that it is an excellent forum for positive reinforcement. Try some of these on for size!

That's an excellent question.

Perhaps that idea would work. Let's try it.

That's a creative way of looking at it.

Not many people would have come up with such an unusual idea.

Terrific idea!

Very interesting thought! Maybe it would work.

I never thought of it that way. Good idea!

That could be just the ticket!

That suggestion makes a lot of sense.

That idea is pretty fantastic.

What a wonderful thought!

That suggestion is quite unique.

That shows you're really thinking.

Let's consider Joe's idea.

Very imaginative!

Splendid!

What a marvelous plan!

Let's consider Sue's recommendation.

Very creative!

Let's give Kim a round of applause for that suggestion.

Very inventive!

Let's follow Tim's line of thinking and see where it goes.

Now why didn't I think of that? Good job.

How did you ever think of such a good idea?

Congratulations on coming up with that solution.

You're very observant!

Your good ideas are popping like popcorn.

That could be just the answer we need.

All right!

That idea shows you're really thinking.

You're quite a **POWERTHINKER.**

Your question shows you put a lot of thought into the problem.

You're really thinking today!

Good going!

That's a pretty awesome idea!

Brilliant idea!

You're very creative.

Great plan!

I knew you could figure out an answer for yourself.

You handled that tough problem very well.

Wow! I'm impressed.

You made a wise decision.

You handled that problem well.

Brilliant!

Jill has the hang of it now.

What an interesting proposal!

This class is full of good ideas today.

See what you can accomplish!

Working together really works.

Well done!

I can't believe all the great ideas you've had today.

Nice job!

Keep up the good work.

That is so outrageous it's contagious!

BIBLIOGRAPHY

Teacher Books

Beyer, Barry K. Practical Strategies for the Teaching of Thinking.
    Boston: Allyn and Bacon, 1987.
Bloom, Benjamin, et al. Taxonomy of Educational Objectives: Handbook 1: Cognitive Domain.
    New York: David McKay, 1956.
Heiman, Marcia and Joshua Slomianko, eds. Thinking Skills Instruction: Concepts and Techniques.
    Washington, DC: National Education Association, 1987.
Raths, Louis E., et al. Teaching for Thinking: Theory, Strategies & Activities for the Classroom.
    New York: Columbia University, 1986.
Whimby, Arthur and Jack Lockhead. Problem Solving and Comprehension.
    Third edition. Philadelphia: Franklin Institute Press, 1982.

Student Books

Anno, Mitsumasa. Anno's Counting Book.
    New York: HarperCollins Children's Books, 1977.
Burns, Marilyn. The Book of Think or How to Solve a Problem Twice Your Size.
    Boston: Little, Brown, 1976.
Geisel, Theodor. Oh Say Can You Say?
    New York: William Morrow, 1976.
Hoban, Tana. Big Ones, Little Ones.
    New York: William Morrow, 1976.
Hoban, Tana. Is it Rough? Is it Smooth? Is it Shining?
    New York: Greenwillow, 1984.
Lionni, Leo. Swimmy.
    New York: Pantheon Books, 1963.
Nozaki, Akihiro and Anno Mitsumasa. Anno's Hat Tricks.
    New York: Philomel Books, 1985.